MORE
SYNONYMS

Shout and yell and other
WORDS THAT MEAN THE SAME THING
but look and sound as
different as loud and noisy

MORE SYNONYMS

JOAN HANSON

Published by
Lerner Publications Company
Minneapolis, Minnesota

FOR
ABBY!

International Standard Book Number: 0-8225-0289-5
Library of Congress Catalog Card Number: 73-11974

Second Printing 1974

syn·o·nym (SIN-uh-nim) A word that has the same or nearly the same meaning as another word. These words are synonyms: *little* and *small; big* and *large; pretty* and *attractive.*

Each pair of synonyms in this book consists of two names for the same thing.

Loud ... Noisy

Sick ... Ill

Angry...Mad

Thin ... Skinny

Empty...Hollow

Friend ... Playmate

Catch . . . Capture

Clumsy • • • Awkward

Laugh . . . Giggle

Insect ... Bug

Picture ... Drawing

Present . . . Gift

Find . . . Discover

Prison . . . Jail

Cover ... Lid

Baby ... Infant

Ache . . . Pain

Scared ... Frightened

Copy . . . Imitate

Order . . . Command

Shout . . . Yell

Wet...Damp

Happy • • • Glad

Cry . . . Weep

Farewell . . . Goodbye

Complete . . . Finish

BOOKS IN THIS SERIES

ANTONYMS
hot and cold and other
WORDS THAT ARE DIFFERENT
as night and day

MORE ANTONYMS
wild and tame and other
WORDS THAT ARE AS DIFFERENT IN MEANING
as work and play

HOMONYMS
hair and hare and other
WORDS THAT SOUND THE SAME
but look as different as bear and bare

MORE HOMONYMS
steak and stake and other
WORDS THAT SOUND THE SAME
but look as different as chili and chilly

HOMOGRAPHS
bow and bow and other
WORDS THAT LOOK THE SAME
but sound as different as sow and sow

HOMOGRAPHIC HOMOPHONES
fly and fly and other
WORDS THAT LOOK AND SOUND THE SAME
but are as different in meaning as bat and bat

British-American SYNONYMS
french fries and chips and other
WORDS THAT MEAN THE SAME THING
but look and sound
as different as truck and lorry

MORE SYNONYMS
shout and yell and other
WORDS THAT MEAN THE SAME THING
but look and sound
as different as loud and noisy

*We specialize in producing quality books for
young people. For a complete list please write*

LERNER PUBLICATIONS COMPANY
241 First Avenue North, Minneapolis, Minnesota 55401

96